MAD'S DAVE BERG LOOKS AT YOU

Written and Drawn by Dave Berg

WARNER BOOKS

A Warner Communications Company

YOU As A Young Person—
When Youth is Stranger Than Fiction

PLANE FACTS

TO ERRANT IS HUMAN

FOR CRYING OUT LOUD

①

PLOP!

②

GOING UP FOR THE COUNT

LOVE THY NEIGHBOR'S

HOW GREEN IS MY VOLLEY

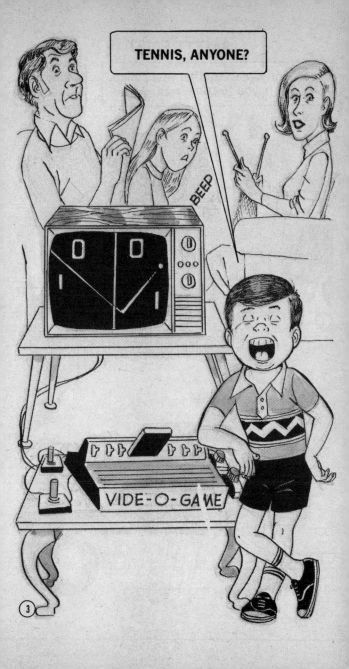

SAFETY FOIST

82 AR

THE LESS THE MERRIER

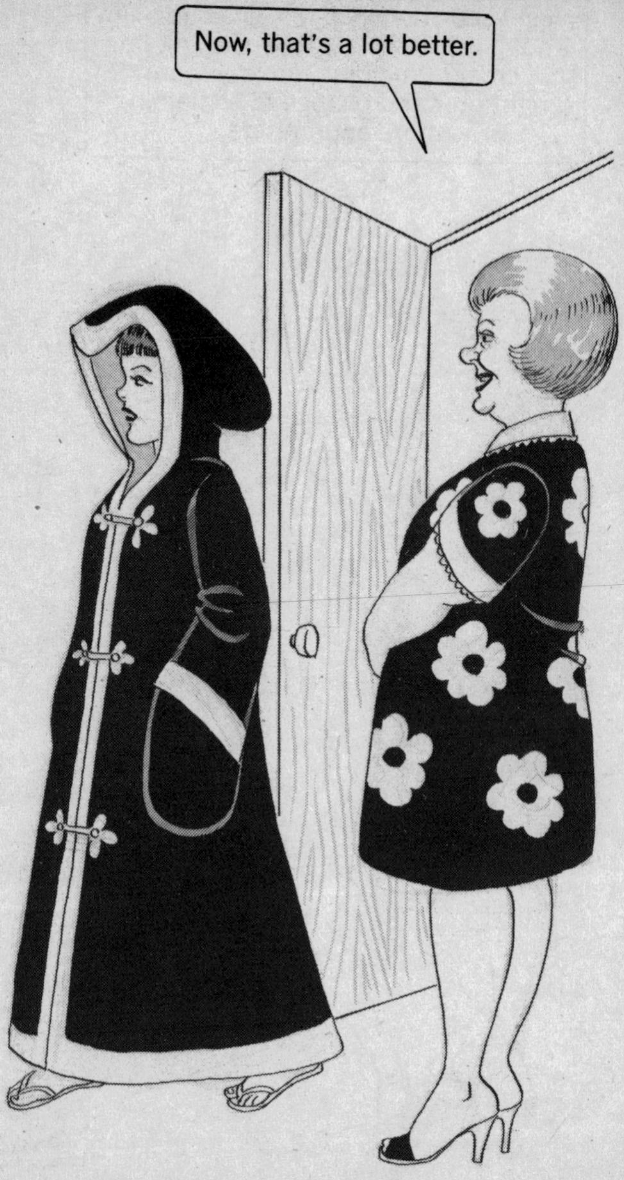
Now, that's a lot better.

CLASS DISTINCTION

PUNISHMENT FITS THE PRIME

This daughter of yours won't **cooperate** with **anything**. She refuses to **set the table** or **wash the dishes** or **take out the garbage**.

①

I've had it with you! March to your room and stay there for the rest of the day!

②

CLOSE ENCOUNTER OF THE WORD KIND

When I first came to this school three years ago, I decided I was going to **make it** with **every girl** in this college.

①

Not only that, I was going to do it in a neat and orderly **system.**

What was your system?

②

(3)

(4)

THE BELLS ARE RINGING FOR ME AND MY PAL

> My parents are always Picky Picky and finding fault with me. They especially bugged me because they said I **use the phone too much.** Which isn't true.

①

> So I decided to run away from home. I broke open my piggy bank, packed a bag and marched down the stairs in a huff.

②

BANKS FOR THE MEMORIES

My Dad is a real rags to riches story. He started his own business by borrowing a **hundred dollars** from the bank.

①

Now he owns a **chain of stores,** with a thousand people working for him.

②

As for **money**—don't ask!
He's so successful that today...

3

...He owes that very same bank a **million dollars.**

4

TELE-PHONEY

SORE WINNER

GRADUWAITED

SEX PACK

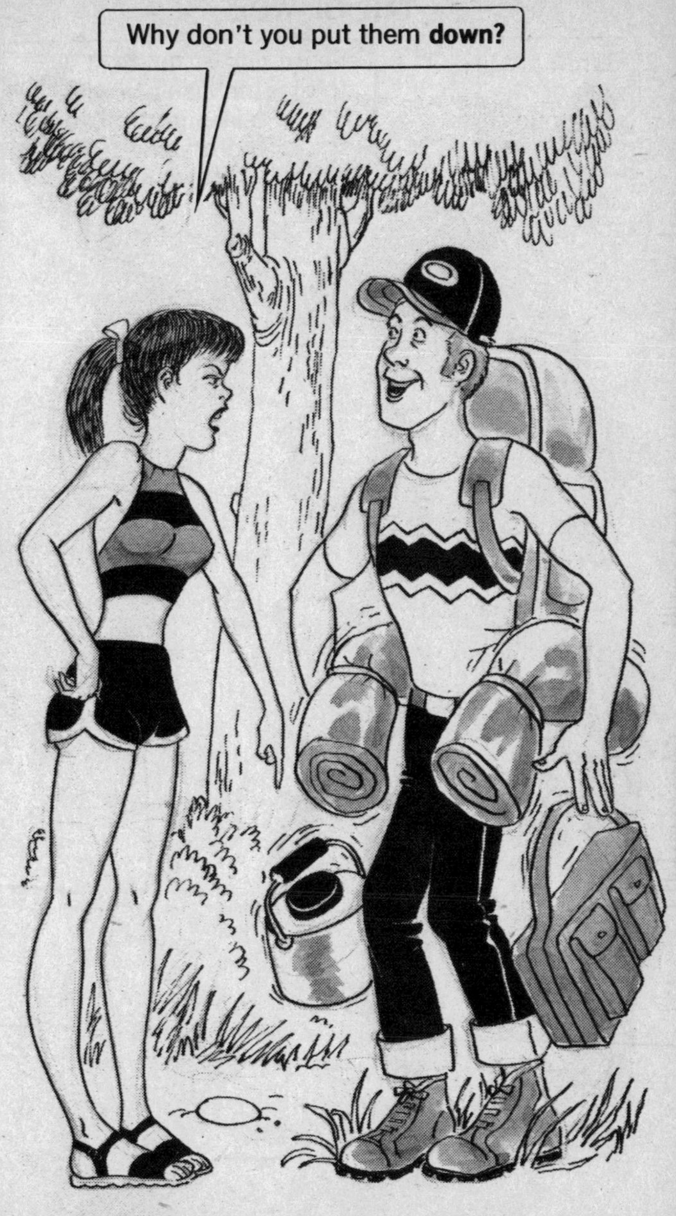
Why don't you put them **down**?

TAIL OF WOE

THE CRASS IS GREENER

Will you look at the Quibbly's house? It's an **eye sore.** The **front lawn** is **overgrown,** spoiling the **symmetry** of the **whole block.**

①

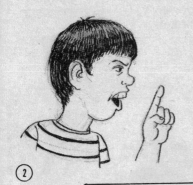

PUTTING YOUR MOUTH WHERE THE MONEY IS

PENMAN - SLIP

JAWS CELEBRE

Well, Patty, this is an extra special day for you. So we have taken you to the **fanciest restaurant** in town. You can order **anything** your heart desires.

①

I want **chewing gum, nuts, candy sweets of all kinds, bread** and gobs and gobs of **peanut butter.**

②

PRIME AND PUNISHMENT

UNREAL ESTATE

YOU As A Married Person—
When You Love, Honor and Disobey

CASING THE JOINT

EASY COME EASY BLOW

A STRAIGHT FLUSHED

WILD BOO YONDER

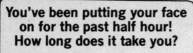

THE FACE THAT LAUNCHED A THOUSAND SLIPS

YES, SIR, THAT'S MY MAYBE

I've been looking over my situation on the job. I observed that my boss is an egotistical tyrant, who doesn't like being contradicted. So I went along with it.

①

I figured in order to make it, one has to survive. So whatever decision he made, I told him it was a **great idea**— even if it **wasn't**.

②

IN A FAMILY WEIGH

TAIL OF TWO CITIES

As mayor of this here fair city, it gives me great pride to announce that while other cities were going bankrupt, we remained **solvent.**

①

We have successfully solved our biggest problem, **welfare.** While Yankee cities like New York didn't have the common sense to know how.

②

TAKING THE HIGH ROAD

I had a terrible **drinking problem.**
I had a **buzz** on **all** the time.
I was using booze as a **crutch** to
help me get through the day.

①

It was **lousing** up my **whole life.**
I was determined to quit. I did it
cold turkey. Now I take it **one** day at a time.

②

A SIGHT FOR SORE GUYS

The woman across the street is a terrible housekeeper. And she has the weirdest friends. And she furnishes her house in early bad taste.

CLOCK WISE

It's 8:00 o'clock **on the dot** and there is good ol' **dependable** Roger Kaputnik.

①

Roger, you are a **remarkable** man. You are **precise** and **self-disciplined**. If you say you are going to be someplace at such and such an hour, you are there exactly at such and such an hour.

②

AUTO MOTIVE

WEDDING GUESSED

3

4

MARITAL BLITZ

BUY AND CELL

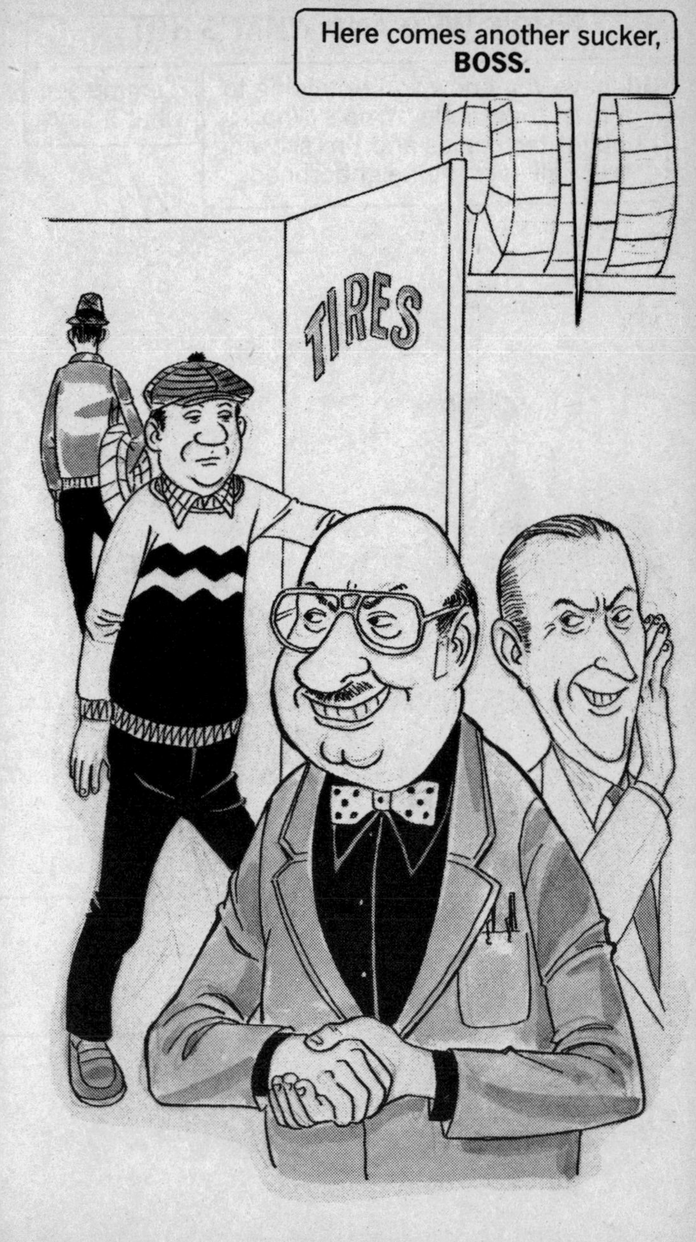
Here comes another sucker, **BOSS.**
TIRES

WHO'S WHO AND WHAT'S NOT

BANGS FOR THE MEMORY

THE PRICE IS FRIGHT

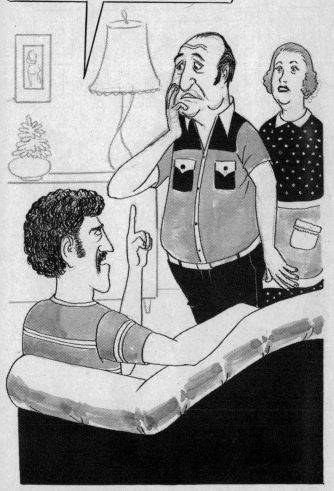

THE LOWEST COME ON DENOMINATOR

EAT DRINK AND BE WARY

STOP LOOK AND WINCE SOME

I look at this magnificent resort we came to and I see the elegance and majesty of the hotel architecture. I look at the setting around it and I see purple mountains in the backdrop. I see emerald foliage and an azure blue sea.

Bernard! You're not looking!

YOU As An Elderly Person—
Growing Old Disgracefully

OUT OF SITE

FOOD FOR NAUGHT

BETTER ATE THAN NEVER

WHERE THERE'S AN ILL THERE'S A WAY

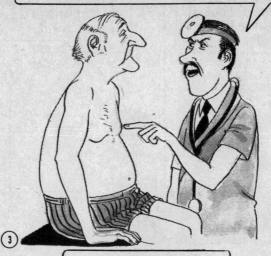

THE BUCK STOPS HERE

SHAPE OF THINGS TO COME

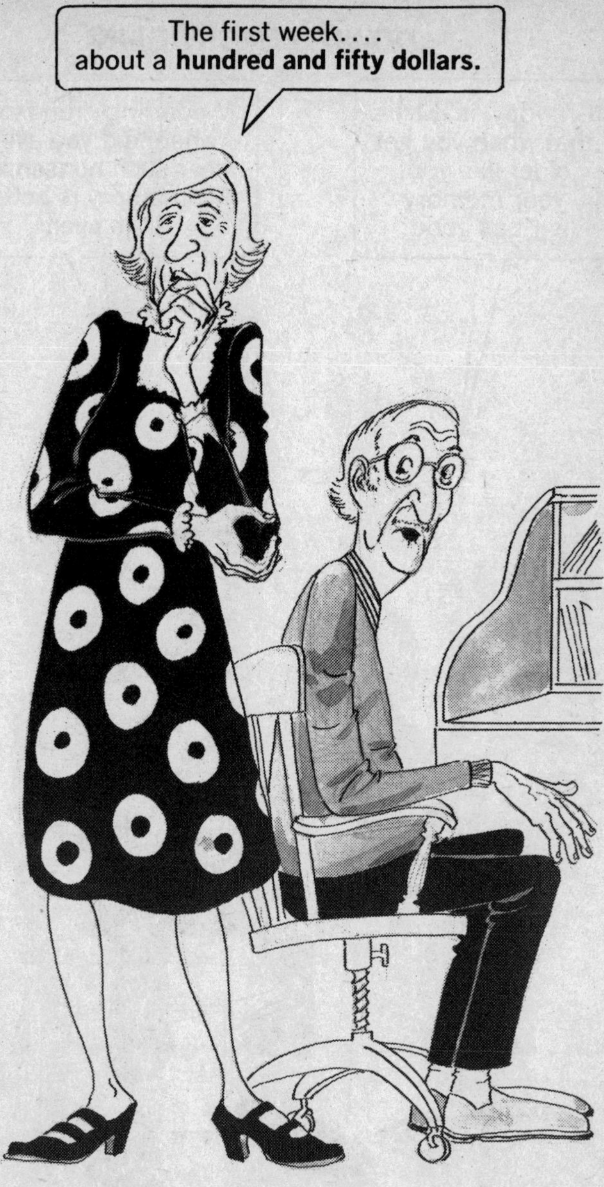
The first week....
about a **hundred and fifty dollars.**

DOWN MEMORY GAIN

HUE OUGHT TO BE IN PICTURES

But this is a **science fiction** show. Those are supposed to be **green beings** from **Mars.**

BEGGARS CAN'T BE LOSERS

Mister, can you spare some money?

(1)

If I gave you money you'd probably go buy some cheap wine and get drunk.

Actually, yes.

(2)

BUY'D YOUR TIME

LINE FORMS ON THE WRONG

This is a stick-up! Fill up this bag with money! If you push the silent alarm I'll blow your head off!
TELLER

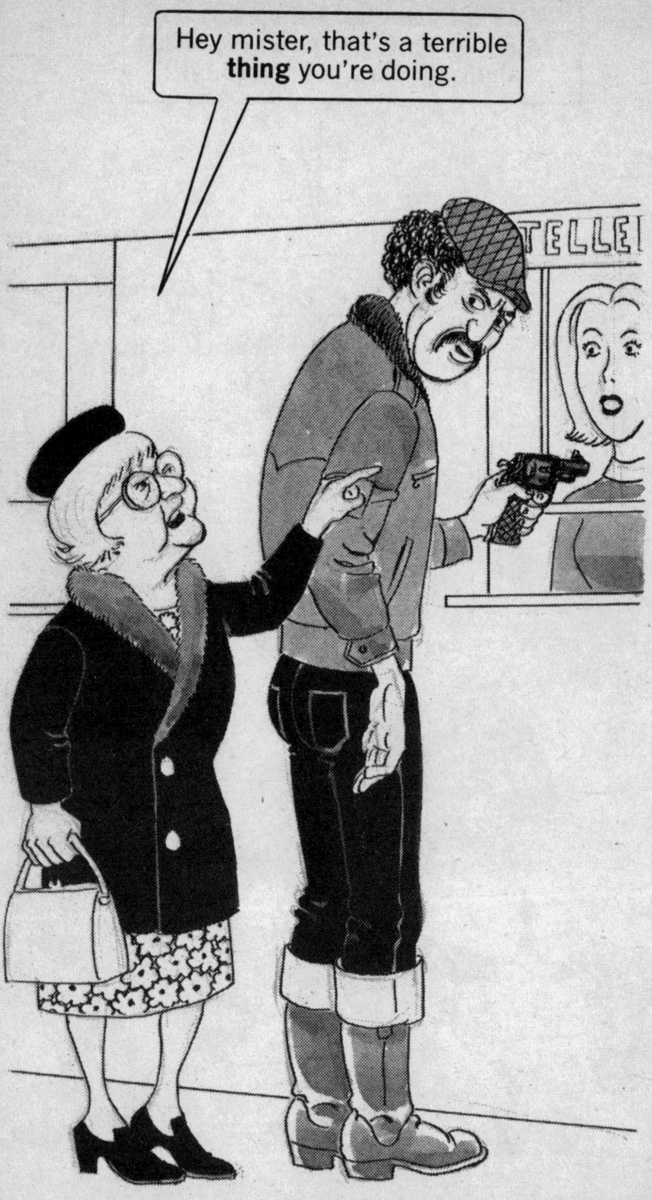
Hey mister, that's a terrible **thing** you're doing.
TELLE

HEAR TODAY, GONE TOMORROW

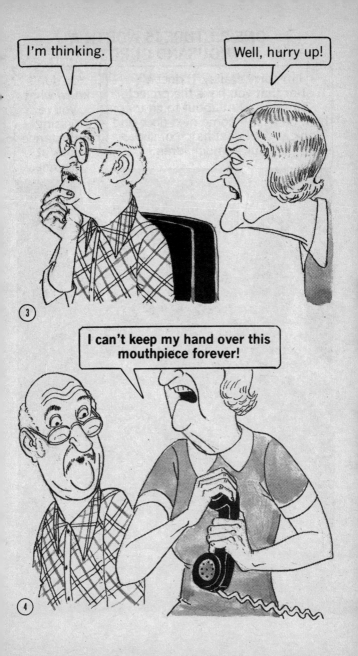

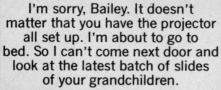

ONE PICTURE IS WORTH A
THOUSAND CURDS.

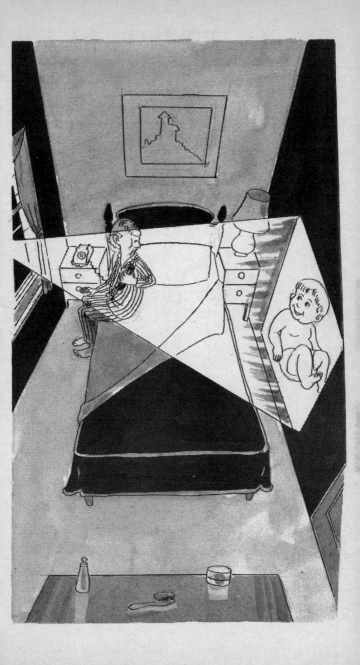

OVER WAIT

ROBBIN' HOODS

SLEEPY TIME PAL

NO ACCOUNT

THE DRESSED IS YET TO BE

That's us before the children grew up and we retired, moved to the sunbelt and bought a condominium.

PRAY TELL

The
Alligator
with the
Lean
Mean
Smile

by Lillian Nordlicht

illustrated by Dennis Hockerman

SCHOLASTIC INC.
NEW YORK • TORONTO • LONDON • AUCKLAND • SYDNEY • TOKYO

ISBN 0-590-33452-2

Reading level is determined by using the Spache Readibility
Formula. 2.0 signifies low second grade level.

Text copyright © 1985 by Lillian Nordlicht. Illustrations copyright © 1985 by Dennis Hockerman.
All rights reserved. Published by Scholastic Inc.

12 11 10 9 8 7 6 5 4 3 2 1   5   5 6 7 8 9/8 0/9
                        Printed in the U.S.A.   11

To my three sons:
Robert, Scott, and Jonathan

Small Hippo
and Big Rhino
lived deep in the forest.

They took
long walks to the river.
They liked to sit
in the water
and splash each other.

One day a stranger
poked his head
above the water.

"Who are you?"
asked Small Hippo.

"And what are you doing here?"
asked Big Rhino.

The alligator didn't answer.
Instead he smiled
a lean,
mean
smile.

Small Hippo moved closer to Big Rhino.
"That smile scares me!"
he said.
"Don't worry,"
said Big Rhino.
"I will take care of you.
That's what big friends
are for!"

"Oh, dear," said Small Hippo.
"He's licking my big toe."

"Just kick up a bit,"
  said Big Rhino.

"Oh me oh my," said Small Hippo.
"Now he's munching on my tail."

"Just stick out your tongue at him,"
 said Big Rhino.

"Oh, no no NO!" cried Small Hippo.

"Now he's nibbling on my ear!"

"I think we'd better get out of here!"
said Big Rhino.
And they did.

But so did the alligator.
He got in front of Big Rhino
and Small Hippo
and blocked their way.

"What's the big hurry?"
  he asked.
"Stay and play a game with me.
  I have some riddles to ask you.
  All you have to do is guess
  the right answer."

"And if we can't?"
asked Small Hippo.
"What will happen then?"

The alligator smiled a lean, mean smile.
Then he opened his jaws wide
and went SNAP!

SNAP

"Oh no!" cried Small Hippo.
"That's awful!"

"Don't worry, Small Hippo,"
 said Big Rhino.
"I am very good at riddles.
 I will answer for the two of us.
 That's what big friends are for."

"Ready?" asked the alligator.

"Whenever you are," said Big Rhino.

"Here goes," said the alligator.
"**What runs but cannot
 walk downhill?**"

"Oh, that's easy," said Big Rhino.
"I know the answer to that one."

Big Rhino thought and thought some more.
"Don't tell me," he said.
"NEVER tell me 'cause I know
   the answer!"

The alligator smiled a lean, mean smile.
"Does that mean you give up?"

Big Rhino sighed.

"I really had the answer on the

tip of my tongue . . . .

But it got away.

So tell me.

What runs but cannot

walk downhill?"

The alligator licked his lips.

"Wait!" cried Small Hippo.
"I think I know the answer!"

"You do?" said the alligator.
"What is it?
  And you'd better be careful
  about what you say.
  **What runs but cannot
  walk downhill?**"

"Is it . . . Is it . . .

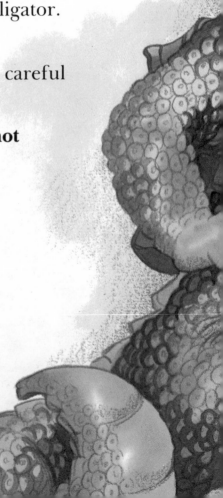

Water?" asked Small Hippo.

The alligator gave him a nasty look.
"It is," he said.

"But here's another one and it's even harder."

Alligator turned to Big Rhino.
"Here is the next riddle.
**What did King Arthur say
to his court?**"

Big Rhino pulled out
the thinking cap that
he happened to have with him.
He put it on and
he thought.
He thought very hard.
Very, very hard.
But it didn't do any good.

"Can't we play Monopoly?" he asked.
"Or capitals of countries?
Or checkers, instead?"

"Time's up!" said the alligator.

And he pulled out some salt and pepper
that HE happened to have with him.

"Hold on!" cried Small Hippo.
"I think I know the answer to
**What did King Arthur say
to his court?**
The answer is . . .

**I want you all to go to
knight school!"**

The alligator kicked the ground.
"That's right," he said.
"But you're not finished yet."

The alligator moved closer to Big Rhino.

"Now here is the last riddle.

Remember!

You MUST answer it correctly.

If you don't . . .

anything can happen.

ANYTHING!

**What is always broken
before it is used?"**

Big Rhino sat down on a rock.
"I think better when I'm sitting,"
he said.

Then he thought and he thought
some more. His shoulders drooped.

"Ready to quit?" asked the alligator.

"I am," said Big Rhino.

"I know the answer," said Small Hippo.
"It's . . .

. . . It's **an egg!**"

The alligator gnashed his teeth.
But then he smiled his lean, mean smile.
"Perfect score for you, Small Hippo.
You may go free.
But Big Rhino didn't answer any
of the riddles.
So that means I get to eat him up!"

Big Rhino groaned.

But Small Hippo thought fast.

"Let's play a game for double or nothing,"
he said.

"I will give you a word puzzle to solve.

If you give the right answer . . ."

Small Hippo gulped.

The alligator's eyes lit up.

"I get to eat the two of you up,
instead of just one?" he asked.

"Is that what you mean by double
or nothing?"

"Exactly," said Small Hippo.

"And if I don't . . .?"

"Then we both go free," said Small Hippo.

The alligator thought for a minute.
Should he settle for one?
After all, one animal in the pot
IS worth two who are not!
On the other hand . . .
TWO would be a REAL treat!

"Okay," he said. "Let's play."

CUL8R ALLIGATOR

Small Hippo found a stick.

He wrote his word puzzle in the dirt.

CUL8R ALLIGATOR

"What does that say?"

he asked the alligator.

The alligator looked at the ground.

"Ha, ha, ha, that's easy," he said.

"Now let me see . . .

Oh, hi-dee-dee, oh, hi-dee-ho.

CUL8R ALLIGATOR

Hmmmm...

CUL8R AL

Hmmmm...

CUL8R ALLIGATOR

Hmmmm...

CUL8R ALLIGATOR

Oh, that's so easy.
Who wants to answer such a
stupid puzzle anyhow."

Without saying goodbye—
the alligator slid back into the water.

"He can't answer it,"
  said Small Hippo.
"Neither can I," said Big Rhino.
"What does it say?"

"It says, **See you later, Alligator**,"
  said Small Hippo.

"Not if I can help it," said Big Rhino.
  And he laughed.
  Then he said, "Now let's get out of here."

As they walked along the forest path,
Big Rhino put his arm
around Small Hippo.
"And may I say that small friends
can be as much help to big friends
as big friends are to small friends?"

"You may," said Small Hippo.
And he put his arm around Big Rhino.

Then together,
they set out to find
a different river to splash in.